THE
A TO Z
BOOK OF
GODDESSES

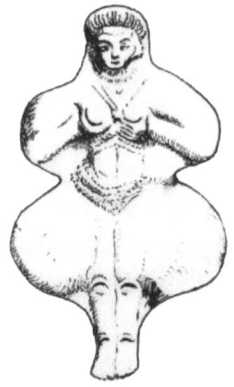

By Michael P. Earney

Copyright Michael P. Earney 2022 All Rights Reserved.
No part of this book may be reproduced, stored in a retrieval system,
or transmitted by any means, electronic, mechanical, photocopying, recording,
or otherwise, without written permission from the author.

ISBN-13: 978-1-941345-94-8 HB
ISBN-13: 978-1-941345-95-5 PB

Cover design by Michael P. Earney

Cover: The Three Graces. A Charis, or Grace, is a goddess.
The three graces, Euphrocyne (mirth), Aglaea (elegance),
and Thalia(youth and beauty) were daughters of Zeus.

Canyon Lake, TX
www.ErinGoBraghPublishing.com

Holy Cow!

Goddesses have had their day
it's over now, they've gone away.
'Tis true most places in the world
in others though, their spell has held.
Goddesses of which you've never heard,
unless you are a Goddess nerd,
continue all their heavenly tasks.
And what are they, a youngster asks?
To protect, to heal, provide so many things,
a cornucopia of gifts she brings.

Goddesses helped folk throughout the day
when in doubt, they showed the way.
How to weave and how to write,
how to love, and how to fight.
And when a person's time had had its run
they led the way to kingdom come.

Each one had her special duty
as Heavenly mother or, as nature's beauty.
Metis, Astarte, and Venus are ones I knew,
though Isis, Athena, and Nut should get their due.
Those goddesses who once ruled the world
were mistresses of all that they beheld.

Myths and legends now are all that's left
their stories show how truly we're bereft.
Were those deities that once guided nations
but figments of Mankind's imagination?
Or, do people, who to goddesses still turn,
hold some truths that we should learn?

M. P. Earney Dec. 2021

Acknowledgements

Thanks to all the goddesses in my life.

Thanks to the North Family.

And a special thank you to Kathleen J. Shields for her

tireless work bringing the book to completion.

Disclaimer

Every effort has been made to trace the copyright holders

and we apologize in advance for any unintentional omissions.

We would be pleased to insert the appropriate acknowledgment

in any subsequent editions of this publication.

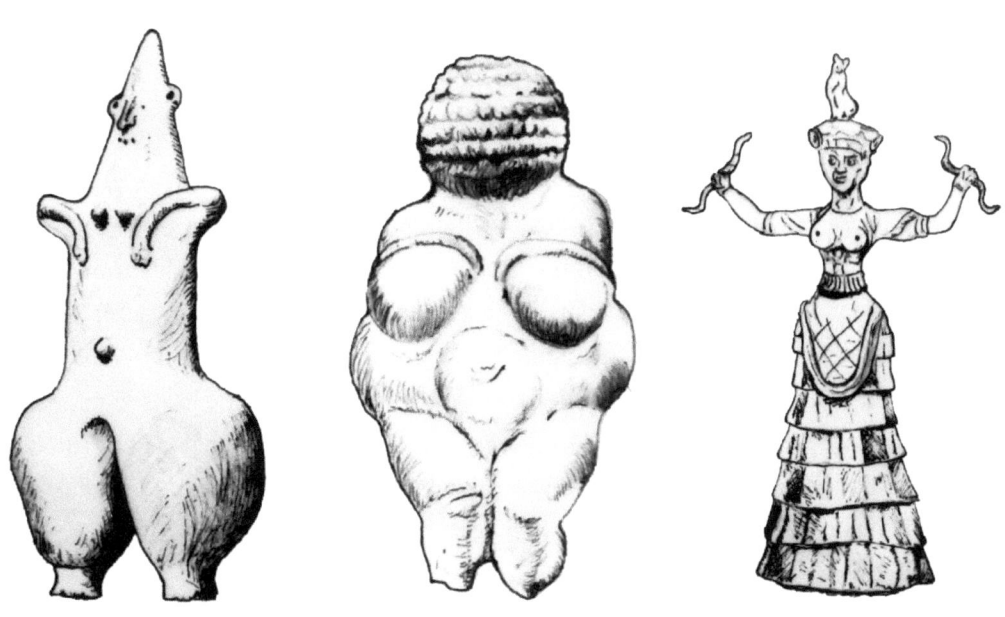

Introduction

When I decided to write the A to Z book of gods it was clear right away that I would have to write an A to Z book of goddesses too. You can't have gods without goddesses even though, in religio-fiction, just like in science fiction, the laws of nature don't necessarily apply. It is generally accepted that the mother goddess started everything. Accepted, that is by those that are not locked into the patriarchal mindset: Genesis 2:7. "The Lord God formed man from the dust of the ground, and breathed into his nostrils the breath of life, and man became a living being." He then went on to make Eve from Adam's rib. In the *Golden Ass* by Apuleius, the Great Goddess says; "I am nature, the universal Mother, mistress of all the elements, primordial child of time, sovereign of all things spiritual, queen of the dead, queen also of the immortals, the single manifestation of all gods and goddesses that are." One creation myth has a goddess giving birth after stepping in the footprint of some god, many deities mixed any number of things with clay to make beings, just like Prometheus, who shaped the human race from a lump of mud, (the goddess Athena had to breathe life into his model). Prometheus' cousin, Zeus, birthed the goddess Athena through the top of his head, having previously swallowed her pregnant mother, the goddess Metis. Metis, the goddess of wisdom, stayed put in the belly of Zeus, providing wise counsel, which he tended to ignore. Like I said, the laws of nature, admittedly not fully understood at the time, don't apply when it comes to gods and goddesses. The exploits of the gods and goddesses, at least those that are no longer around, don't have the consequences they once had. Still, there are millions of people around the world who profoundly believe their lives are ruled by deities who demand prayers, gifts, sacrifices and particular forms of behavior. Although the idea that a divine mother goddess, ruling over matriarchal tribes was the original way of things has been questioned, it is clear that as societies evolved and deities proliferated, goddesses played an equal if not greater, part in the lives of humans. Some goddesses took male consorts for a year simply to fulfill their paternal duties, after which they were often sacrificed, those that were spared sometimes applied for equal status and, if granted, ultimately usurped the leading role, (just like a man). The attributes, and roles of the goddesses were often simply taken over by the gods. Gender being flexible a lot of the time. Similarly, we see the role of a god or goddess in one religion being replicated in the religion of a neighbor or a later civilization. This happened so many times that we have to remind ourselves that the needs and concerns of people all over the world were much the same, the need for a nurturing mother being at the forefront. The duplication of the roles that those gods and goddesses played reflects the commonality of human concerns.

Goddesses were not only loving mothers, they could be vengeful, unforgiving and destructive. Every aspect of life was under their control and continued that way until the transition from a matriarchal to a patriarchal system, that took place over centuries eroding the status of women in the world, a process that continues to this day. Patriarchies came to dominance and the role of the female was diminished to the point where today, in some societies, a woman has little or no say in how she chooses to live. While some matriarchal societies still exist and some religions are still practiced that have active goddesses, in Western societies the very idea of a supreme goddess ruling over our lives would never arise in the minds of men, or women, for that matter.

The goddesses had and still have in some societies, a profound effect and echoes of the effects, of those no longer with us, can be seen and felt even today, hidden perhaps, and hard to discern, but we will seek them out and bring them to light. Goddesses that are worshiped to this day will be examined as will be those, thought to be long gone, but who continue to have their followers and exercise some control over the minds of many who otherwise, would never acknowledge a belief in such things. Certainly, the role they played in the formation of the world, their gifts to humans and the ways in which their existence shaped how we think and act can only give us a better insight into who we are.

> You can safely assume that you've
> created God in your own image when
> it turns out that God hates all
> the same people you do.
>
> Anne Lamott

A
IS FOR
AMATERASU

Amaterasu, Goddess of the Sun, also known as Amaterasu-Ōmikami, born from the left eye of Izanagi, the creator god. Her name means "Shines from Heaven". The longer one means "the great and glorious Kami who illuminates from heaven". Another is "Ōhinume- no- muchi-no- kami" "the great sun of the kami" (kami are spirits or "holy powers"). Tsukuyomi, Amaterasu's brother emerged from Izanagi's right eye, he reflects his sister's light as the moon. As a married couple, they rule the day and the night. They separated after Tsukuyomi, out of disgust, killed Uke mochi, the goddess of food, at a banquet when she spat fish into the sea, game into the forests, and then started pulling crops out of her rectum for him to eat. Amaterasu couldn't accept his behavior and that is why day and night are no longer seen together. A contest between Amaterasu and her younger brother Susanoo got out of hand when Susanoo went on a rampage, he was the storm god, after all, destroying much of Heaven and earth. Ashamed for her part in the quarrel, Amaterasu hid in a cave, plunging the world into darkness and chaos. She wouldn't respond to direct appeals to come out and almost a year went by before the gods put on a big party outside her cave. The noise and all the activity got her attention. Ōmoikano, the god of wisdom and intelligence, had an Eight-Fold Mirror setup outside. When her curiosity got the better of her, she looked out, the mirror reflected her light and as she stared, wondering if they had somehow found another goddess as brilliant as she, Ōmoikano removed the stone blocking the entrance to the cave and Amaterasu's light reentered the world. She apologized for her acts; Susanoo was banished to earth and she returned to heaven. Susanoo did redeem himself. An eight-headed dragon had eaten seven sisters and was about to eat one more, Susanoo got the dragon drunk on saki, and cut off its heads with a magic sword he found in the dragon's tail. He sent the sword to Amaterasu as a token of submission. Together with her mirror and jewels, it forms the Japanese Imperial regalia. Susanoo married the girl. Amaterasu directed her son Amano-Oshiho-mimi to go down and rule the earth. When he stood on the bridge between Heaven and earth and saw what a mess the earthly deities had made of the place, he said, "No thanks". It took years of various gods' efforts before they were able to convince Oho-Kuni-nushi, the earthly ruler, to give up his sovereignty and take over the underworld instead. Amano-Oshiho-mimi refused the job for the second time so, Amaterasu sent her grandson Ninigi down. With the Imperial Regalia, given him by his grandmother, Ninigi established justice and harmony on earth. His grandson was Jimmu, the first Emperor of Japan. Jimmu then, was said to be the great, great, great-grandson of Amaterasu. Under Shinto, the religion of Japan established by the Emperors, all the Emperors could trace their ancestry back to the Sun Goddess. Known as the land of the rising sun, Japan's state flag has a red sun disc centered on a white background. The Imperial standard has a sixteen petal chrysanthemum on a red background. As noted in "The A to Z Book of Gods", the Emperor Hirohito after surrendering to the US forces, ending WW II, was allowed to continue as Emperor in order to ensure the Japanese armed forces would comply with the peace treaty. Hirohito subsequently denied that he was a god so his successors cannot claim to be related to Amaterasu and Japan is now no longer ruled by a deity.

Cool Fact: Having put up with her brother's shenanigans with great forbearance, the final straw that caused her to head to the cave was when she sat on her throne to preside over the Feast of the Flowers, she was sickened by the smell of excrement, he had voided under her seat. Enraged, she took to the cave and set that rock-door in place.   **What other Goddess names start with A?**

B is for Brigid

Brigid, Bridgit, Birgit, Bridid, Brig. Goddess of Healers, Poets, Smiths, Childbirth; she was said to lean over every cradle but she was on hand for the birth of farm animals too. Inspiration; not only for poets but musicians, artists, and craftsmanship. Fire and Hearth; the fire part made her the patroness of smiths and metalworkers. She was the patron of warfare. Brigands were once the soldiers of Brig. Lots of titles, lots more names too; Brigantia, Brid, Briginia. Brigdu. She was the goddess of wells and rivers. Brigid's Well in County Kildare, Ireland is a famous landmark. Its water is said to have healing powers making her revered as a healer, too. All this, and there's more to come, suggests she was an archetypal Triple Goddess, something we will go into later.

Brigid arrived in Ireland along with the Tuatha De Dannan a Celtic people who occupied much of Europe and invaded the island around the third century BC. In the battles to gain control, both her father and son were killed. Her mourning at the death of the boy is said to be the inspiration for the tradition of "Keening" the form of grieving carried out by women at funerals and wakes. Keening can also be heard in the music of Ireland which aims to evoke the purity and emotion of her mourning that made her the goddess of music and inspiration.

Danu, the mother goddess for whom the Tuatha De Dannan were named, was Brigid's mother, little is known about her and after their arrival in Ireland, Brigid rose to the position Danu had held. Aside from all her other roles, she was the Goddess of Spring. Brigid originally meant "Rising" or "High" or "Bright". In her robe of sunlight and with her flaming red hair she ruled over the summer months. The festival of Imbolc, held roughly midway between the winter and summer solstices, was when Brigid came back to earth bringing light and fertility. Her Holy day is the beginning of spring, prayers of supplication that she provide the warmth and care the newly born needed were fervently made. At the summer solstice, wells were visited and offering made to her.

Given the paramount place she held in the lives of the Irish it's only natural that when Christianity came to the island, she be worked into the system somehow. She became St. Brigid, the patron saint of Ireland. St. Patrick, the other patron saint of Ireland, credited with bringing Christianity to Ireland, had been a slave there before returning as a missionary. Although some believe there was a slave girl named for the goddess who became Ireland's first nun and ultimately, St. Brigid; that she once hung her cloak on a sunbeam, might suggest that her story is no more likely than the goddess one. St. Brigid's cathedral in Kildare, built in 1223, is the site of the feast day of St. Brigid, also known as Mary of Gael, it takes place on February 1st., Imbolc. Considered to be the beginning of spring, Imbolc was a pagan festival, it, and all the other activities associations with the goddess Brigid, visiting holy wells, prays for homes and livestock, the time of divination, all passed on to St. Brigid.

Get thee to a nunnery!

Cool Fact: Maman Brigitte, with her fair skin and red hair, wife of Baron Samedi, the spirit of death in Voodu, stands out in a religion formed by black African slaves when they arrived in the Caribbean. The Catholic influence on Voodu and the character of Maman Brigitte points to one thing. She gives the same maternal care to the dead that the goddess Brigid and her saintly counterpart gave to the living.

What other Goddess names start with B?

C IS FOR COATLICUE

Coatlicue, Co-at-li-cuwee. Aztec Earth Goddess. She was a major deity who, among other things, gave birth to the moon, or was that her son? We'll never know for sure. We do know that she was both a creator and a destroyer. She was sweeping the steps at her shrine on top of Mount Coatepec when a ball of hummingbird feathers fell from the sky. She caught the feathers in her apron and became pregnant with Huitzilpochtli. Stay with me now, because it gets complicated with different versions of what happened next. Her daughter, Coyoixauhqui, convinced her mother had dishonored the family, gathered her four hundred brothers, determined to kill her. The instance she is killed, her unborn son emerges from her womb fully grown and armed, he kills most of his siblings including Coyoixauhqui. Version number two: As the family assembles to do the deed, one of the four hundred, Quanitlicuc, warns the unborn child, Coatlicue immediately gives birth to the fully grown Huitzilpochtli. Armed with his darts, his blue dart thrower, and shield, he kills Coyoixauhqui, cuts her up and throws her body parts down the mountainside, except for her head which he throws into the sky where it becomes the moon. He pursues the brothers mercilessly, those that get away become the star deities of the southern sky.

A large heavily carved stone disc showing Coyoixauhqui's dismembered body was found at the foot of the Templo Mayor, on the side dedicated to Huitzilpochtli, in Mexico City in 1978, graphically recording the event and supporting the theory that the temple was built to replicate Mount Coatepec. Coatepec held a major place in the legends of the Aztec even though it is not known which mountain it was exactly. Just to confuse matters more, some sources have Xocitlicue, the goddess of fertility and younger sister of Coatlicue, as the mother of Huitzilpochtli and Quetzalcoatl.

The ten-foot tall basalt statue of Coatlicue, now in the National Museum of Anthropology in Mexico City, depicts her in her most terrifying form, found in 1790 it was so upsetting that it was promptly reburied. It was dug up again then reburied, as the authorities were dismayed when indigenous people came to worship it. When Alexander von Humbolt visited Mexico City it was dug up again for him to take plaster casts then finally placed in the museum. She has a severed head, replaced by two coral snakes, representing flowing blood; a reference to the version where Huitzilpochtli springs from her body when his siblings beheaded her. She has a necklace of hearts and severed hands and a large skull pendant. Her hanging breasts tell us she was an older woman, past childbearing age. Entwined rattlesnakes form her skirt, her hands and feet are large claws for ripping up humans before she eats them. Not exactly the image we might have of a loving mother, but snakes symbolize fertility, rebirth, transformation, and immortality. Something we do thank Mother Earth for.

Another interpretation says that at the time of creation, Coatlicue and four of her sisters voluntarily sacrificed themselves in order to set the sun in motion. They left only their skirts from which they were eventually resurrected. The statue, therefore, represents the resurrected Coatlicue.

Cool Fact: Cōātl "snake" gives us Coatepec "snake mountain" home of her temple and birthplace of Huitzilpochtli. Quetzalcoatl "plumed serpent" Cihuācōātl "snake woman" and Coatlicue "she with the skirt of snakes." **What other Goddess names start with C?**

D IS FOR DEMETER

Demeter. Barley Goddess, Goddess of agriculture, fertility, and sacred law. The cycle of the seasons is explained in the story of her search for her daughter Persephone. One version goes like this: Persephone was sent out to color all the flowers of the world, Hades, the god of the underworld, swooped down and carried her off to his domain. Demeter's unsuccessful search for her, which is covered in many other stories, left her extremely upset, to the point that she withheld all her gifts and the world turned into a frozen desert. All the gods went to Demeter and told her she should get over it as people were starving. Her reply was that the earth would not bear fruit again until her daughter was returned to her. Zeus, who was her brother and the father of Persephone, sent Hermes, who ran all the messages of the gods, down with orders that Persephone be sent back. Hades reluctantly obeyed but gave Persephone four or six pomegranate seeds to eat before she left. Demeter and Persephone were happily reunited but when she told Demeter about the seeds she knew that she could not keep her daughter. Each seed represented one month she must spend in Hades henceforth. One of the rules of the underworld. Rhea, the oldest of the gods was sent by her son Zeus to deliver this message: "Come my daughter, for Zeus, far-seeing, loud thundering, bids you come once again to the halls of the gods (Olympus) where you shall have honor, where you shall have your desire, your daughter, to comfort your sorrow. As each year is accomplished and bitter winter is ended. For the third part, only the kingdom of darkness shall hold her. For the rest, you shall keep her, you and the happy immortals. Peace now. Give men life that comes alone from your giving." Demeter brought forth her daughter, the radiant maiden of spring with all her fruits and flowers, aware that she would die with the winter and rise again each spring. One scholar proposed another version in which the four months Persephone spent in Hades were the dry Greek summer months when drought threatens the crops. Versions of this story are found in many religions and this isn't the only version the Greeks knew. It came from early agrarian societies predating the Mycenean Greek period, (approximately 1600-1100 BCE). The Eleusian Mysteries that were carried out each year were a reenactment of the Demeter and Persephone story and continued on for about two millennia with crowds flocking to participate: It was a major festival and the only requirements for participation were, the initiate had never committed murder, and wasn't a "barbarian," meaning unable to speak Greek. That was it. Initiates were sworn to secrecy, on pain of death, so almost nothing is known for sure what happened during the days of the rites that were spread throughout the year. Drawing on knowledge of similar rites practiced by agricultural societies of the Middle East and Crete has given us a pretty good picture of what took place during the Mysteries. There were Processions, feasts, and sacrifices overseen by priests. At one point in the processions, obscenities were shouted in commemoration of Baubo, the old lady goddess of mirth, who had tried to cheer Demeter from her sorrow by telling her dirty jokes. An all-night feast, full of dancing and merriment, capped off the Mysteries. It took place in the field that, supposedly, was where the first grain was grown after Demeter had taught humanity agriculture. The festivities were described as "orgies" so Kykeon, the drink of water, barley, and pennyroyal given to the participants may have served to prevent pregnancies as pennyroyal was known to stimulate menses in small doses, and also served as an abortive in high doses. Pennyroyal is toxic and has caused death in users. It has been speculated that the barley in Kykeon may have been parasitized by ergot, a fungus with LSD-like alkaloids, causing the revelatory states experienced by some participants.

Cool Fact: Demeter's emblem, the red poppy grew alongside barley, her gift to humanity, the poppy's bright scarlet might have stood as a symbol of resurrection. It has also been speculated that during the Eleusian Mysteries opium made from the poppy was used.

What other Goddess names start with D?

Ēostre, Ōstara. Goddess of Spring and rebirth.

Ēostre and any number of other spellings of her name comes from the Proto-Indo-European languages that evolved into Germanic languages and on into any number of dialects. Mercian, Northumbrian, Kentish, and West Saxon dialects were spoken in the independent kingdoms of England before it became a unified country. Each of these entities and the many others of England, Scotland and Wales, developed their own versions of the myths and legends that carried the history of all that got them to the lands they called home. The Spring Goddess was a common deity to all people, being one aspect of the Triple Goddess. She is the young, pure Maiden, the representation of innocence, growing and blossoming, seen as the flowers, trees, and grasses put on their spring faces when birds and animals produce their young. She represents the bounty of nature that will bring the harvest of Mother Earth to sustain them through the dead of winter represented by the old Crone. Whether Ēostre was one spring goddess behind all those names has put philologists to a lot of work but studies have turned up many place names associated with her. A Dawn goddess, "H^2ewsós" and another, "Austrō" have been cited as the origin of Ēostre and Ōstara. However, Ēostre is a name found only in the work of the Venerable Bede. Bede was a Benedictine monk in the 8th century. The monastery in Northumbria where he spent most of his life, had a large library and he corresponded with scholars in many countries so he may have had access to information not generally available. Bede wrote that Ēosturmonath the equivalent of April, was when Anglo-Saxons had held large, weeks-long feasts in honor of Ēostre. A tradition replaced by Pascha, when the resurrection of Jesus was celebrated. Since the spring celebrations associated with the spring goddess had not died out, "Easter", as his celebration, became the tradition in England; another example of Christianity co-opting pagan holidays. To eliminate any hint of Ēostre, the first Sunday after the first full moon after the Spring Equinox was dubbed "Easter." When better to celebrate the miraculous return to life of all that had lain dead during the long winter months?

The traditional Easter activities, such as the egg hunt, egg rolling, egg tapping and the egg dance, are clearly adopted from Pagan fertility rites, eggs being symbols of fertility and purity. The Easter Bunny harks back to her too, as rabbits and hares are recognized symbols of fecundity.

Cool Fact: Ōstara Nutrient Recovery Technologies, Inc. is a Canadian company specializing in resource recovery from wastewater and sewerage sludge treatment. Their technology dewaters sludge to produce struvite,(a material that deposits and builds up in pipes carrying sewer water), in the form of crystalline pellets that are sold as fertilizer under the name "Crystal Green." Ēostre would surely approve.

What other Goddess names start with E?

F
IS FOR
FREYJA

Freyja. Goddess of love, passion, fertility, sex, war, death, the afterlife, and gold. The most beautiful and most popular of all the Norse gods. Freyja is linked to the planet Venus, Friday, apples; her colors are, red, gold and fire. Her symbols, two cats and the hawk.

"Where shall wisdom be found and where is the place of understanding?" Under the apple tree, by pure meditation, of a Friday evening, in the season of the apples, when the moon is full."

The Norse Edda's, two 13th century Icelandic literary works, are the source of most of what we know about Norse mythology. The Teutonic gods, while common throughout Northern Europe, went by different names according to location, for example, Woden became Odin, Donar was Thor. Freyja and the goddess Frigg were often confounded. There were two races of gods too, the Aesir and the Vanir. Frey was the most important of the Vanir and Freyja was his sister. The following are edited down versions of stories from the Edda's that feature Freyja. One of Freyja's most prized possessions was her gold necklace. How she got the necklace is a long story but in brief, she saw it being made by four dwarf metal-workers and offered money and jewelry, they wanted none of it. Their price? She must spend one night with each one of them. She accepted. When Loki, the trickster god, saw it he decided he would steal it. He got into her bed-chamber by turning himself into a fly. Freyja was sleeping in such a way that he couldn't reach the clasp so he changed himself into a flea and bit her so that she moved, he removed the necklace and walked out of the chamber. He hid the necklace under a reef in a far-off sea, taking the guise of a seal to get there. Heimdall, another Scandinavian god, known mostly for being tall and handsome with pure gold teeth, was a sworn enemy of Loki, he turned himself into a seal and after a fight with Loki, took the necklace and returned it to Freyja. Freyja's beauty attracted many gods who tried to obtain her favors either freely or by force. These stories, often involving Loki, told in poetic or song form, may have had some deeper meaning or they may have been purely for entertainment. In another, Thor's hammer was stolen by a giant named Thrym. Loki went to find out where it was hidden but Thrym had it deeply buried. He agreed to return it only if Freyja would be his wife. Thor's hammer being very important to all the gods, they asked her to accept the proposal. She angrily refused. Loki then convinced Thor to borrow Freyja's cloak of hawk feathers and veiled, go with him to Thrym. He almost discovers their plot but is so excited about the prospect of having Freyja that he gets the hammer and places it on his prospective bride's knees, as was the custom, Thor grabbed it and slew Thrym and his whole band of giants. Again, is there a hidden moral or social message there? Or no more than a bawdy tale told while sitting around the fire of an evening.

The popularity of Freyja as the goddess of fertility continued long after the demise of the gods, despite the efforts of the Christian church to defame her. Together with her magic necklace, the Brisingamen, symbol of the earth's fruitfulness, the important role she was thought to play in the lives of farmers and herders, continued well into the 19th century, in Sweden, people were still attributing sheet lightning to Freyja striking a flint with a steel to produce a spark so that she could see if the rye was ripe.

Cool Fact; The question of whether Freyja and Frigg were a single goddess or whether both are versions of another goddess of the Proto-Germanic period remains and scholars continue to work on it.

What other Goddess names start with F?

G
IS FOR
GANGA

Ganga, goddess of purification and forgiveness. She is the personification of the Ganga (Ganges) river in India. Fair complexioned, wearing a white crown, she rides a Makara,* usually portrayed as a crocodile, holding a water lily in her right hand and a lute in her left. When portrayed with four hands she carries a water pot, a lily, a rosary, and one hand is held in a protective position. She is the only living goddess in the Hindu Pantheon.

The Ganges, her sacred river, is believed to wash away all sins and grant the devotee salvation. Ganges is the Westernized name. Known as the Ganga to Hindus, it rises in the Himalayas, at 1,509 miles long, it is the third-largest river in the world by discharge. Of the three Holy cities that draw millions of pilgrims for their "holy dip," Varanasi draws the most. The ashes and remains of those cremated at Varanasi's ghats are thrown into the river, the bodies of Holy men are thrown directly into the river as are those of pregnant women, those who committed suicide, had leprosy, chickenpox, or were bitten by snakes. The poor, who couldn't afford cremation, and children under the age of five, are also thrown into the river. Varanasi pumps millions of untreated sewage into the river daily. 400 million people live close to the river and many rely on it for bathing, washing, and cooking water. Despite the high risk of infection, millions take their dip to cleanse themselves of sin and hope to obtain salvation. As the mother of humanity, Ganga's river is considered to be the one means by which the souls who immerse in it, whether as ashes or bodies, are liberated from the cycle of life and death. As with all gods and goddesses that have been around for a long time, Ganga has multiple stories. In one, she was the daughter of the King of the Himalayas, when she grew up she was taken up to heaven by the Devas, where she became a river. An accident caused her waters to flow out of heaven, washing across the lotus feet of Lord Vishnu, it settled in the abode of the Lord Brahma before descending to earth. That it not destroy Mother earth, Lord Shiva held it on his head, slowly releasing it to form the river Ganges to meet the needs of the people of India. In some traditions she is married to Vishnu but, after getting into scuffles with his other wives, Vishnu gives her to Shiva. Even though as a river, she can be destructive, as a goddess she has no destructive or fearsome aspect. She is essential to Hindu worship and culture wherever in the world Hinduism is practiced. Her divinity is everlasting, so long as the river survives. Global warming is having its effect on the Himalayan glaciers that feed the river bringing the increased risk of flooding but, if they disappear, water supplies will be in peril. The monumental disaster that this would produce is of great concern and is being addressed on some levels but, corruption, ignorance, indifference, and willful inaction are cause for even greater concern. Ganga will no longer be a living goddess.

Cool Fact: * A Makara is the sea-creature that Ganga traditionally rode, it took many forms, generally a combination of a terrestrial animal, a deer, or an elephant with a hind part of a fish, seal, or snake. It is thought that the South Asian river dolphin (now endangered), the dugong, and even depictions of the Chinese dragon may have contributed to its image originally. The Makara that Ganga is more often seen riding these days is either the Asian water monitor or the Marsh crocodile.

What other Goddess names start with G?

Haumea is the Hawaiian Goddess of fertility and childbirth. She is the oldest and the most important god of Hawaii. The sister of the gods Kāne and Kanaloa. With Kanaloa, she parented the war god Kekaua-kahi and the volcano goddess Pele. Pele was born the normal way but the rest of her brothers and sisters were born from various parts of her body. Four were born from her head. In some versions of the story, Pele came out of her mother's mouth as a flame. That would make more sense, she being the goddess of the volcano. It's also said that Pele found a wide area of land and released water over it until only the tops of its mountains showed above the water, these are the Hawaiian islands. Haumea also had children with her father; her daughter, Hi'iaki, according to some texts, was fathered by her brother Kāne . Able to transform herself from an old woman to a young girl, through the ages with the aid of her magic stick, Makaki, she returned to her homeland periodically to marry one of her offspring. Sleeping with her children, grandchildren, and great-grandchildren, she brought about generations of humans. There were other ways in which she could propagate, by becoming the Breadfruit tree she grew leaves and bore fruit. The Banana was also her tree. Eventually, when her child Ki'o was born she was exposed as the ancient she was. In a huff, she took off and left humanity behind. Before this, however, when she was visiting the daughter of a chieftain who was experiencing a painful childbirth, she discovered that humans only gave birth by Caesarian. Appalled, she created a potion from the Kani-ka-wi tree (*Spondias dulcis*) which enabled the mother to push out the baby naturally.

The story of Haumea is very much like that of La'ila'i. Both come from the land of the gods and La'ila'i's children by Ki'i, "come from the brain", just as Haumea's were said to. La'ila'i was also a shape-shifter. Haumea was also confused with Papahānaumoku, the earth mother who was married to Wākea, the sky father who were parents of the ruling chiefs of Hawaii.

When a great famine struck Hawaii the trickster god Kaula, tricked the other gods into letting him take all of their food to give to the people, making him their hero. Haumea was blamed for the famine and Kaula got a magic net with which he trapped Haumea and killed her.

Now distinctly Hawaiian, the Hula was introduced to the islands by Polynesians, the original settlers there. Originally a religious dance performed by trained dancers to promote fecundity, honor the gods, or to praise the tribal chiefs, it has become a favorite entertainment for tourists. The traditional grass skirt, the wearing of the lei, and the use of other plants in the dance connect the dancers to the environment and to its fertility. In 1820 New England missionaries compelled the dancers to change their short hula skirts for long dresses. No doubt there was a whole lot more about Hawaiian ways they disapproved of.

Cool Fact: Telescopes in Hawaii were involved in the discovery of a faint, distant dwarf planet. In 2008 the International Astronomical Union,(IAU) announced they had named that planet, the 5th known dwarf planet in the Solar System, "Haumea." The planet's two moons were named for her two daughters, Hi-iaka, the sea goddess, and Namaka, goddess of Hula dancers.

What other Goddess names start with H?

I IS FOR **IXCHEL**

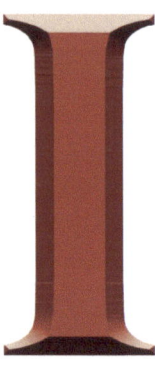

Ixchel- *Eeshel* is another triple goddess, we will find many of these. As a Maiden, she is the goddess of fertility and medicine. She often has a rabbit companion, they being a symbol of fertility and the moon, (the Maya were not the only people to see a rabbit on the moon) or a fish, another fertility symbol. Her snake headdress connects her to sacred medicine. As a Mother, she is connected to weaving and the moon. She sends patterns to weavers in dreams and remedies to healers. She has no snake headdress in this aspect, she is concerned only with raising, healing, and caring for her own children. As an old crone, she again has the snake headdress, crossed bones on her dress, and was sometimes shown with claws instead of hands, now being the goddess of medicine, healing, midwifery, and keeper of the souls of the dead. Like so many gods and goddesses, she may have derived some of her aspects from other forgotten goddesses. As moon cycles determine harvest time she was most venerated during the month of 'Zip', August through September, when she carried a jug to pour water onto the crops. As Chak Chel "large Rainbow" she caused a great flood that destroyed the 3rd Creation, preparing the way for the next age, the 4th Sun. The island of Cozumel (island of Swallows) and Isla Mujeres (island of women) in the Caribbean off the coast of Yucatan, were both pilgrimage destinations for married women to pray for procreation. Mayan women were expected to go there at least once in their lives. There were many shrines to Ixchel on the islands and on Cozumel at least one had a large statue where a priest would hide and deliver oracles. The most generous women donors would get better "readings" than others. As the goddess of childbirth and weaving, her spindle as the motion of the entire universe determined the sex of the child to be borne.

Said to be hopelessly in love with Itzamna, the all-powerful ruler of the heavens and day and night, she followed him across the sky, unknowingly causing strong raging tides and failed crops, she then had to run back to right the chaos she had caused. Once married, she bore him thirteen sons. She was also linked to Votan, the Tzeltal god of war and drumming and the chief god of the Mayan Pantheon. Together, on the orders of the gods, they were said to have founded the city of Palenque. From the tiny amount known of Votan the Spanish, always looking for a way to assert that the civilizations found in the Americas came from the Old World, developed the following scenarios; Votan was a.) Noah or a descendant of Noah, b.) A white European, c.) A Phoenician, d.) Builder of the Tower of Babel, e.) Came from the lost city of Atlantis. Alexander von Humbolt, never shy about offering his opinion, noting the similarity between the name Votan and Woden/Odin suggested that the Germanic gods could have been transported across the oceans at some time in the distant past.

Cool Fact: The classical glyph for Ix Chel is still unknown and the name Ix Chel was only given to her in the 16th century. In her "old Crone" stage, she corresponds to the goddess O who was an old jaguar goddess involved in midwifery.

What other Goddess names start with I?

 IS FOR JESTAK

Jestak, *Jastak,* Goddess of the hearth and Lifeforce, protector of children and birth-giving women. Jestak is a goddess of the Kalasha people who live in a remote mountainous region of the Hindu Kush in northern Pakistan. The Kalasha are an anthropologist's dream come true having retained their ancient, nature-centered beliefs in the face of unremitting hostility from their neighbors. In 1895 the Afghan emir decided the Kalasha would convert to Islam or be wiped off the face of the earth, in the same manner as happened around the world, when the followers of one religion decide that all others are wrong, Kalasha temples and icons were destroyed, priests were murdered and boys were kidnapped for conversion, (the Kalasha of Afghanistan were converted to Islam). Islamists, the Taliban being the latest, continue to threaten the ways of the Kalasha even though the Pakistan Supreme Court has declared it illegal to attack other religions on the grounds of personal belief. The Kalasha produce wine, from grapes grown in their fertile valleys, upsetting their Muslim neighbors even more. The few remaining traditional Kalasha stubbornly carry out their very complex and esoteric rituals, overseen by Shamans who play their flat round drums and using a variety of psychopharmaca, Ceremonies dedicated to a wide array of gods and goddesses are carried out in accordance with their calendar throughout the year. At New Year, Elders sit on the mountain tops, (home to the elves and fairies who aid in the hunt and the killing of enemies) to witness the dawn and the first light strike the valleys below. People stay inside until the declaration of the New Year is made at which time goats and other animals are sacrificed to Jestak and their blood is sprinkled that she may show mercy for the people's sins and bring purity to their hearts. Great emphasis is given to the pure and the impure, anyone that may have been exposed to the impure must be cleansed with the smoke of a burning juniper branch. Women are considered impure during their period, they gather in the Jestak Han, or Bashaleni lodge, while they are menstruating, birth delivery is carried out there and the ceremony of initiation into the clan for young girls is also conducted there.

Alexander the Great passed through the area on his way to India and the making of one of the largest empires of all time. The occurrence of fair hair and blue eyes among the Kalasha has given rise to the claim that the Kalasha are descendants of the Greeks. While there may well have been some dalliance, and certain practices like, wrestling and shot-put are carried out there, DNA studies suggest they are descendants of stone-age Siberian stock.

Cool Fact: Rudyard Kipling's book, "The Man Who Would Be King" is based on the reputed connection between the Kalasha and Alexander's soldiers, although it takes place between the Kalasha of Nuristan in Afghanistan. The 1975 film, *The Man Who Would Be King* starring Sean Connery and Michael Caine is based on Kipling's book.

What other Goddess names start with J?

Kokyangwuti, *Koh-kyang-woo-tee,* Kahyangwuti, Koyangwuti, etc. "Spider Woman". "Spider Grandmother". In Hopi mythology she appears as an old woman or as a spider. She is called upon for advice, to cure illness and ailments. Various Native American cultures in the South West have such a character. The Navajo insist Spider Woman taught the Navajo women how to weave which, in a way she did, as Hopi women, enslaved by the Navajo, showed them how to make wool into yarn, to dye and weave it. The Hopi have more than one creation story involving Spider Woman. Sotuknang, or Tawa, the Sun God had created the world but there was no life, so he created Spider Woman and gave her the task. She made two beings from clay, twins, one she sent to put his hands on the earth to solidify it. The other she told to send out sound so that the world would become an instrument of sound, tuned to the voice of the creator. Then she created all the plants, birds, and animals. Once Sotuknang saw their work he declared it ready for human life so Spider Woman created four males and four females. In another version, Tawa had his nephew, Sotuknang create the universe under his directions. Another story has the twins coming from the union of Tawa and Huzryiwuhti, the always bride of Tawa but, since she was the result of Kokyangwuti dividing herself, you could say that it was the Spider woman anyway. She and Tawa divided themselves in order to have more gods to share their labors. Confused yet? How about this; Tawa and Kokyangwuti brought people into existence by singing. "I am Tawa, sang the Sun God. "I am Light. I am Father of all that shall ever come." "I am Kokyangwuti." the Spider Woman crooned. "I receive Light and nourish Life. I am the Mother of all that shall ever come." After a lengthy process, singing all the while, humans breathed and lived. Since Kokyangwuti lived underground as a spider, humans spent the first three worlds underground until she led them into the 4th World (today's world). That was quite a journey, as you can imagine, once here, the Hopi divided into Clans with Kokyangwuti choosing a different creature to lead each clan. She told them that the women of the clan would build the house and the family name would descend through her. She would be the homemaker and man would build the kivas, (each clan's underground place of council and worship), make weapons, and provide the family with game.

Even though there are no images of Spider Woman, she is described as, 'Of shining beauty dressed in a soft white woolen top over a blue skirt, on the left side of which was woven, in red, yellow, and green, a band of squash blossoms and butterflies, bordered with bands of black. She wore a heavy necklace of turquoise, shell, and coral. Pendants of the same hung from her ears. She wore gleaming white skin boots.' Much the same as the traditional dress you might see Hopi women wearing today during festivals or celebrations.

Cool Fact: Princess Leia in the "Star Wars" series of films wears her hair in the same style as Hopi girls who are ready for marriage. The bundles of hair curled on each side of their head are called, Squash blossom whorls or Butterfly whorls.

What other Goddess names start with K?

L IS FOR LILITH

Lilith. The dangerously beautiful Mother Goddess of childbirth, children, women, and sexuality. In the Talmud and in the book of Genesis we read; "So God created man in his own image, in the image of God created he him; male and female created he them." What!? Wait a minute! Yes, they were created at the same time, from the same clay, and since they were equal the female refused to be subservient to the male. That was Adam, who insisted that she was fit only to be in the bottom position. Seeing that argument was going nowhere, she flew off. Adam went to God and told him she had left. God sent three angels off to bring her back but she said no. That first woman coupled up with the archangel Samael,(he supposedly took the form of a serpent to tempt Adam and Eve) and said she wasn't interested in the Garden of Eden. So, God made Eve from Adam's rib. Lilith was that first female. The Kabbalah has some different versions of events, in one, Lilith is created before Adam. In another, Adam and Lilith were attached until God separated them. Yet another has Lilith emerge as a spontaneously divine entity or, she appeared on the first day of creation when God said "Let there be light". Then again, Lilith and Samael were married and born at the same time as Adam and Eve, both pairs were Hermaphrodites. Lilith forced herself on Adam and gave birth to demons, on and on. The difficulties of translation and interpretation of ancient texts, or fragments of texts that are already translations or mistranslations of even older, lost writings have frustrated scholars for centuries. Lilith, however, very quickly became demonized, her name, Lilith or Lilit, was said to mean, "night creature", "night monster", "Night Hag", or "Screech Owl". She became a sexually wanton, dangerous demon who steals babies at night. Thousands of bowls have been dug up that were buried upside down, under houses, or in the corner of the home of the recently deceased that were intended to protect the owner from the evil influence of Lilith and any other malevolence that might be out there. Amulets, inscribed with the names of the three angels dispatched by god, were also worn to keep Lilith at bay. She was the bogeywoman before there was a bogeyman. Of course, Eve got her fair share of condemnation for tempting Adam and getting them thrown out of Eden, to the detriment of all mankind. Lilith's story might be seen as the beginning of the demise of goddesses. As Adam said, woman's place was on the bottom, man's on top.

Still, the fascination with Lilith has prevailed through the years, in Goethe's "Faust" there is this exchange; Faust: Who's that there?
Mephistopheles: Take a good look. Lilith.
Faust: Lilith? Who is that?
Mephistopheles: Adam's wife, his first. Beware of her.
Her beauty's boast is her dangerous hair.
When Lilith winds it tight around young men she doesn't soon let go of them again.
Dante Gabriel Rossetti wrote a sonnet, *Lilith* to accompany his painting *Lady Lilith* that he expected to be his, "Best picture hitherto".
Cool Fact: Wiccan's and other occult groups who believe in the supernatural and magic, hold Lilith in great esteem, worshiping her as a goddess of independence and as a sex goddess.

What other Goddess names start with L?

M

IS FOR
MNEMOSYNE

Mnemosyne. Goddess of memory, one of the Titans her parents were Uranus (Heaven) and Gaea (Earth). Cronus, the father of the Greek gods and leader of the Titans was her brother. Mnemosyne knows everything, past, present, and future. In *The White Goddess,* Robert Graves wrote, in reference to her, "One can have memory of the future as well as of the past. Memory of the future is usually called instinct in animals, intuition in humans." Like many of the Greek goddesses, Mnemosyne was impregnated by Zeus, her cousin, on this occasion disguised as a shepherd, sleeping with her on nine consecutive nights so that she gave birth to the nine Muses, goddesses of the arts, science, literature, and inspiration. Although Zeus' reason for impregnating Mnemosyne was strictly selfish, he wanted to be sure all his great victories and decisions would not be forgotten, without the muses inspiring poets, songwriters, and historians, all of history, myths, and legends, before the written word, would be unknown to us. All storytellers invoked the Muses before reciting, beginning with Mnemosyne, to refresh their memory. Without reference books or Google, those tasked with memorizing tribal history, the ancestors, the celebration of seasonal events such as, times of planting, hunting, the gathering of plants for food, medicinal as well as poisonous ones along with all the other information necessary to the survival and well-being of the people underwent years of schooling and utilized any number of techniques to aid in their recollection. Memory aids, or devices, included knotted ropes, beads, stones, shells, chants, pilgrimages, certain locations where inscriptions, made over time, were essential aids, the stars in the sky held stories. Songs and chants that might take days to perform, served to remind everyone who they were and where they came from. Performance spaces were 'tuned' to aid the performers. It has been suggested that stone circles, found around the world, similarly served as memory aids. Just as a singer may not recall the words of a song they have sung countless times, until they hear the first chords of the introduction, knowledge keepers also needed that little nudge. Temples dedicated to her and statues of her in other temples received offerings from those hoping that she would help them remember visions they might receive in dreams when they awoke. You know how hard that can be. Her counterpart in Hades was Lethe, the goddess of forgetfulness and oblivion. In Hades souls were forced to drink from the river Lethe in order to have no memory of their past life when they were reincarnated. However, there was a pool in Hades called Mnemosyne, drinking from that restored the memory of one's past life, halting the cycle of rebirth. Those that drank the waters of that pool went to the Elysian Fields to spend eternity in comfort and peace. Some might say that spending eternity remembering everything in our past could be rather uncomfortable. Your choice.

Cool Fact: Mnemosyne and mnemonic both derive from *mnemē* Greek for "remembrance, memory". A mnemonic phrase is intended to help one remember a list of things in their correct order; "Super Heroes Must Eat Oats" gives us the Great Lakes from largest to smallest: Superior, Huron, Michigan, Erie, Ontario. "My Very Educated Mother Just Served Us Nachos"? The order of the planets out from the sun: Mercury, Venus, Earth, Mars, Jupiter, Saturn, Uranus, Neptune.

"The quick brown fox jumps over the lazy dog" is a pangram, it includes all the letters of the alphabet, not a mnemonic, strictly speaking, but, I think that Mnemosyne would approve.

What other Goddess names start with M?

N IS FOR NINHURSAG

Ninhursag, Ninkharsag, Ninharsag, Nintina. Sumerian Mother Goddess of the Gods and the Mother of Men. Having a part in the creation of divine and mortal beings she is one of the oldest and most important deities, although she replaced an earlier Mother Goddess, Nammu. Her Ziggurat, (temple) was adorned with a lapis lazuli serpent, the symbol of medicine and healing. Her personal symbol was the umbilical cutter, signifying her role as mother goddess. Known by a variety of names she was wife/consort to various gods bearing their children. She was the half-sister of Enlil, and Enki with whom she bore a daughter who then also bore a daughter with Enki, that daughter was them raped by Enki. Ninhursag removed the semen from the girl's vagina and planted it in the ground. Eight new plants appeared which Enki then ate, becoming sick, Ninhursag then cured him by taking the plants into her body and giving birth to eight new deities. Another version has Enki hoeing the plants and uncovering the heads of Mankind, then Ninhursag completes their birth. She was thought to form children in the wombs of women and to provide food after they were born. As with all the early stories of the gods there are many and conflicting versions, lost parts, and difficulties of translation. That fact has given rise to altogether different translations of the texts. In one of these, the gods did indeed come down from the heavens and Ninhursag, the chief medical officer, together with Enki were called upon by the lesser gods, who were carrying out all the hard labor, to produce a worker, one who could take over such tasks. After all she was the "Womb Goddess" and the, "Mother of all children." Taking the egg of one of the primitive beings they called "The black heads" she fertilized it with the sperm of one of the gods, and replanted it in the womb of the ape woman. Months later she shouted, "I have created- my hands have made it." The first artificial insemination, as far as we know. Later, after ape women's eggs had been fertilized they were placed in the womb of "birth goddesses". Later still, after some 50,000 years of genetic engineering, some of the gods began to take an interest in the females created in this way and started procreating with them, and here we are. If you ever wondered whether the woman you adore is a goddess, well, in part, she is.

Cool Fact: As male deities came to dominate the "Cradle of Civilization" as Mesopotamia is known, goddesses who represented the left side, and left itself, were looked upon as representing the dark side. With the rise of patriarchy, females and the goddesses became the symbol of negativity, even of evil. Ninhursag suffered the same fate and by the end of the Assyrian Empire she was no longer worshiped.

What other Goddess names start with N?

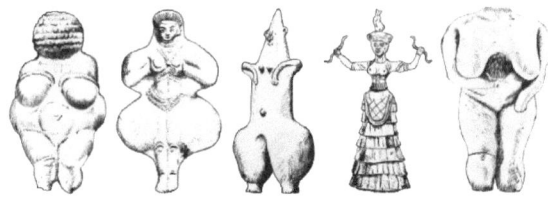

IS FOR
Olokun

Olokun, Yoruba goddess of the sea, Goddess of wealth and abundance, goddess of death she is also the goddess of rebirth and renewal, so women pray to her to conceive. From the dark watery womb of the deep sea new life springs constantly. Like many female deities, she is associated with the dark or left, since no light penetrates to the bottom of the ocean where she lives. She owns all the oceans and all the riches they possess. Darkness is the realm of dreams and secrets of the unconscious, that is her world. From there, together with Oya, deity of the wind, she creates storms and floods. Olokun is an **orisha**, these are spirits sent to earth by the supreme creator, Olodumare, to teach humans how to be successful. Once incarnated as humans they live ordinary lives but, being divine they have great wisdom and power. In the Ifa branch of the Yoruba religion the opposite is believed; there, **orishas** are divine beings who once were humans who gained their divinity through spiritual growth and accomplishments while living on earth. Kind of like saints in the Roman Catholic religion. Among the Yoruba of Benin, Osanobua is the creator and supreme god and the father of Olokun who rules all bodies of water, bringing prosperity and fertility, however, close to the coast Olokun takes a male form, in the hinterland she is female. Often depicted as a beautiful black mermaid she is also symbolized by the mud fish. Red coral is linked to her; growing on the remains of dead ancestors, it is an apt metaphor, the reefs that coral form purify the water and provide shelter for other sea creatures and plants.

When the gods wanted to create land on the planet for human habitation, Olokun was at first hesitant but, finally, she agreed that a small part be turned into solid land while she still would reign over the greater part, the sea. Now, with plastic and all the other debris of mankind raining down on her head, she may regret her decision. Let us hope that the vast, incredible ecosystem of the oceans she rules can combat the enormous strain and save us from ourselves.

Cool Fact: In Brazil, Candomblé, combining African and Roman Catholic religions, does equate **Orisha,** or orixas as they are known there, with Catholic saints. Rituals involving drumming, dance, and singing are carried out to encourage orixas to possess one of their members. Through this individual, they might then communicate directly with a deity.

What other Goddess names start with O?

P

IS FOR PELE

Pele, pronounced *Peh-leh*. Hawaiian goddess of volcanoes and fire. Creator of the Hawaii islands. Daughter of Haumea, the goddess of fertility and childbirth and one of the most important gods of Hawaii, read all about her under H. Descended from Papa, the Earth Mother, and Wakea, the Sky Father, who were descendants of the supreme beings, Pele is known as "The earth-eating woman", "She who shapes the sacred land", and often referred to as "Madam Pele", out of respect.

Scholars suggest that the first settlers of Hawaii came from the Marquesas Islands and that they fled into the mountains when the second wave, from Tahiti, came. Known as the Menehune and the "little people" in mythology, spirits that only came out at night. The arrival of the first Polynesians has been given as early as 124CE to 700 or 800. New findings give a much later date of c. 1025-1120 with the settlement of all the islands coming about c.1219-1266. Pele was ahead of everyone, being chased from her home by her sister, Nāmaka a sea goddess, on account of her fiery, disruptive ways. Legend has it that Pele tried to create fires on a number of islands on the way from Tahiti to Hawaii, that her sister caught up with her and killed her, however, her spirit made it to Halema'ma'u a fire pit in the caldera of Kilauea, on the Big Island of Hawaii. Kilauea is one of the most active volcanoes on Earth. Pele is also a "goddess of the hula" the dance invented by her other sister, Hi'iaki. Dances dedicated to Pele are often performed in a way to represent her intensity and the movement of volcanoes. Hula dances, offerings, rituals and prays are performed on the rim of the caldera where she resides and Pele appears in the steam emitting from the volcano, her body is the lava flow. She has added some 500 acres of new land with her eruptions. She can also appear as a white dog, an old lady or, a beautiful young woman.

Pele's Hair is formed when strands of molten basaltic glass from lava fountains or cascades, stretched by wind are carried into the air. Falling to the ground they form mats of 'hair'.

Pele's Tears are black, solidified lava drops often found on the end of a strand of Pele's hair.

Pele's Seaweed is formed when water and boiling lava meet. As the water boils and turns to steam, bubbles form in the thin sheets of lava. When the bubbles burst, the brownish-green sheets resemble seaweed.

The London Missionary Society started working on the natives of Tahiti in the 1800's, in 1817 a reformed ironmonger named John Williams began spreading Christianity throughout Polynesia though only the external forms of the religion were performed, more out of fear of the missionaries than of conviction. In 1893, Queen Liliuokalani was forced to abdicate and she was finally arrested for treason. The United States of America annexed the islands and in 1959 Hawaii became the 50th State but, Pele still rules.

Cool Fact: The Caribbean island of Martinique has a volcano named Pel'ee, in May 1902, the Volcano erupted killing 30,000 people in less than two minutes.

What other Goddess names start with P?

Q**Qadshu.** Goddess of Sexuality, Sacred Ecstasy, and Fertility. Quadshu, Qadashu, Qadesha, Qadesh, Qudshu, Qedeshet, Kedesh. The Semitic root, Q-D-S, meaning "holy" or "blessed" was used as an epithet for a number of goddesses in Syria, the lack of vowels in Semitic means you have to supply your own, hence the variations. Qadshu, meaning the holy one was given to Athirat, the great mother Goddess of the Canaanites. In time, however, Qadshu became a Goddess, independent of all those other 'holy ones.' The cult that grew around her involved the ritual of the sacred marriage that we see in a number of different religions; the goddess takes a consort for a fixed period of time after which he might be killed, 'sacrificed,' or retired. During the seasonal rite of Qadeshah, (the 'holy ones' or 'religiously clean or pure ones') also known as vestal virgins, temple priestesses, or acolytes, gave themselves to devotees who came to the temple, taking the role of the goddess to reenact the sacred marriage. In Patriarchal times these 'holy ones' came to be described as prostitutes which they were not in the sense we use the word today. Faint echoes of the practice may be found in the Roman Catholic church where virgin Sisters take to a nunnery and give themselves to God.*

During the New Kingdom in ancient Egypt, she was added to the pantheon of gods under the name Qadesh. She rode nude on the back of a lion holding her emblems of fertility, the lotus flower, a papyrus, or snakes. Her hair hung in two curls to her shoulders or she might be shown wearing a Hathor wig since she was similar to Hathor the Egyptian Goddess of Sensuality. She became known as "Mistress of All the gods", and, "Lady of the Stars". There are those that reject the idea that Qadshu existed before she appeared as Qetesh (Qadesh) in Egypt, the evidence is considered to be faulty at best. Little is known about her duties or functions. Since she does not appear in any royal cults it is suggested that the title 'Mistress of the Stars" meant that she was a goddess of commoners and therefore not important to the ruling classes. It is also possible that she arrived in Egypt along with Syrian slaves that the Egyptians were in the habit of periodically securing.

Cool Fact: A frontal nude, as Qadesh was portrayed, was uncommon in Egyptian art which lends credence to the idea that she was a Syrian Goddess before she became an Egyptian Goddess.

*Nikah Mut'ah or, 'temporary marriage' Muhammad appeared to have condoned it in the Quran at least, during the hadith. The Sunni believe it should only be practiced at certain times while the Shia continue to allow it. Scholars disagree over the interpretation of the passage in the Quran and the argument as to whether 'temporary marriages' are legitimate goes on.

What other Goddess names start with Q?

R IS FOR **Rhea**

Rhea; *ria.* Greek Goddess of the Earth. As we see in so many religions rape and incest play a big part. Rhea was the daughter of Uranus and her son Gaea, and was sister to a number of other important gods and goddesses. With her younger brother, Cronus she gave birth to more important deities. That was quite a task as Cronus, upon learning that one of his sons would dethrone him, took the precaution of swallowing each of them as they were born. Having given birth to her son Zeus in Crete she wrapped a stone in a blanket and presented that to Cronus. Zeus was raised secretly and once he was grown up he fulfilled the prophecy, after getting his father to throw up his now fully grown siblings who helped to overthrow the Titans who supported Cronus. Zeus became the supreme authority of the earth and top dog on Mount Olympus. As the mother of Zeus Rhea elevated to being "the mother of the gods." From Crete, where fertility rites dedicated to her were performed, her worship spread throughout Greece. Temples were dedicated to her in many places and many claimed to be the birthplace of Zeus. As time went by, she was conflated with other goddesses and was known under different names in different parts of the country, even her name was given different meanings. In an Orphic myth, when Zeus started coming on to her, Rhea turned herself into a serpent, undeterred, Zeus turned himself into a serpent, and Persephone was born of that union. Elsewhere Persephone is said to be the daughter of Demeter and Zeus who, according to the great poet Hesiod, was Zeus' sister. The story of Melanion and Atalanta is a good example of how the actions of one goddess were attributed to another; Aphrodite helped Melanion to win the hand of Atalanta but, when he omitted to thank her, Aphrodite caused them to become so mad with lust that they had sex in the Temple of Rhea, or Cybele, where they had stopped to rest. Rhea, or Cybele, was so offended by their lack of piety that she turned them into lions. Those lions are seen pulling the chariot of Rhea or accompanying Cybele. Even in this age of mass communication and 24hr. Coverage, stories can get very different interpretations. In stories of the gods, there are no "facts" per se so just enjoy the story. It is known that Rhea, was often translated as, "ease" for the comfort and ease that she provided to women during childbirth; that she healed the madness of one of her grandchildren and that she raised Dionysis after his mother, Semele died (Zeus was the father of Dionysis so, it was all in the family). Rhea was also skilled in wrestling. How Rhea became known as a virgin goddess is hard to say but, in the 5th century the Roman Emperor Zeno considered it appropriate to re-dedicate her temple in Byzantium, later Constantinople, now Istanbul, to the Virgin Mary. In addition to being the Great Earth Mother, she is associated with the Milky Way and is said to live at the center of the Galaxy.

Cool Fact: The **pilos crown**, a high cylindrical crown worn by goddesses of the Ancient Near East and Anatolia was adopted by the Greeks for their Mother goddesses Rhea, Cybele, and Hera, which may have contributed to one being mistaken for the other.

What other Goddess names start with R?

S IS FOR SEDNA

Sedna. Mother Goddess of the Deep, also known as the Mistress of the Sea. The numerous Inuit groups throughout Canada and Greenland know her by a variety of names, "Big Bad Woman" being one of them. Her story, handed down orally through the centuries, like her names, appears in a number of variations. In one, her father is Anguta, the creator god and supreme being or, he is the god of the dead. Then again, he may have been a mere mortal. As the daughter of the god Anguta, she is a giantess who, in great hunger, attacks her parents. In another, she spurns the suitors her father finds for her and marries a dog. In another, after rejecting all the hunters in her village her father gives her to an unknown hunter for some fish. When she wakes up in a large nest on a cliff the hunter reveals his true form, a great bird spirit. Her father tries to rescue her, with mixed results. A different bird spirit kidnaps her in another version and takes her to a floating ice island, her father's rescue attempt fails there also. In a version from Baffin Island Sedna is at sea with her family in their kayak, when a storm comes up, they blame the storm on her and throw her overboard. In all the legends, whether thrown over or falling over, when she tries to climb back into the kayak her fingers are cut off, or freeze off. Her fingers become seals and walruses, the puffed-up frozen ones become whales, she sinks to the bottom of the ocean, grows a fishtail, and marries a sculpin, a fish that belongs to the **Cottoidea** family then takes command of the animals of the sea. Still, today, hunters worship her and make offerings to her that she release the sea animals when they are hunting. In order to placate her, she can be temperamental, a shaman may have to wash and braid her hair,(something she can't do, with no fingers) so that the sins of humans, all of which wind up in the sea and ultimately in her hair, and the creatures tangled up there, will be released so that humans can eat again.

> That woman down beneath the sea,
> She wants to hide the seals from us.
> These hunters in the dance house,
> They cannot mend matters.
> They cannot mend matters.
> Into the spirit-world will go I,
> Where no humans dwell.
> Set matters straight will I.
> Set matters straight will I.
> Inuit song.

Cool Fact: Discovered in 2003 a minor planet, about half the size of Pluto, was named for Sedna. It is in the coldest known region of our solar system (minus 400 degrees Fahrenheit). I think that even the goddess would lose more than her fingers there. **What other Goddess names start with S?**

T IS FOR TLAZOLTEOTL

Tlazolteotl. Aztec Filth Goddess. What! We have noted elsewhere that there is a goddess for everything but filth didn't come to mind. So let's explore this a little more. Tlazolteotl (Tlacolteotl) does mean "Filth Deity" In Nahuatl, the Aztec language. As you may know, the Aztec were big on personal cleanliness so we see that she was the goddess of steam baths and purification. As such, she forgave the sins of lust and sexual misdeeds taking upon herself the filth (sin) of those who committed adultery and the diseases caused by sinful behavior. Interestingly, she was thought to inspire sinful desires and to cause sexually transmitted diseases. Similarly, the god of the bible, particularly in the old testament, in righteous anger would visit mankind with plagues of various kinds to bring them back in line and relented after receiving prayers and supplications. It was only in her middle age when she absorbed all those sins, as a young maiden she was a carefree temptress, then the goddess of gambling and uncertainty, finally, as an old hag, she preyed upon the young and innocent. These distinctly different aspects led to her being thought of as four sisters of different ages. Sacred knowledge, being the province of initiates and the chosen few, who were sworn to secrecy, is mostly responsible for much of the confusion found in beliefs, rites carried out in deliberately obscure language, orally transmitted, kept the true nature of the beliefs from the majority. What little did leak out was usually incorrect, based on rumor or misunderstanding. It's possible that Tlazolteotl was a Huaxtecan goddess adopted by the Aztec, adding another layer of confusion.

During the eleventh month of the Aztec calendar, equivalent to September 2nd-21st of the Roman calendar, a harvest festival called Ochpaniztli, dedicated to Toci and Tlazolteotl, included in the ceremonies, ritual cleaning, sweeping, and repairing, the casting of corn seed, dances, and military displays. Toci "our grandmother" during the harvest festival was honored as "Heart of the Earth". In their duties, Toci and Tlazolteotl were virtually interchangeable though Toci joined the Aztec pantheon thanks to a gruesome interaction between the Mexica (before they became the Aztec) and the Culhua. If you care to go down that rabbit hole, be my guest.

Cool Fact: Tlazolteotl was depicted with dirt or excrement around her mouth and nose, symbolizing her ability to ingest the sin and, in so doing, purify the sinner. During the sacred rituals, *tzin* in Aztec, performed only once in a person's life, a priest would listen to the person's confessions and decree the penance required, based on the severity and nature of the usually elderly, confessor's sins. The rituals included offerings of "liquid gold" (urine), and gold or, as it was called by the Aztec, teocuitlatl, "excrement of the gods".

What other Goddess names start with T?

U IS FOR UKE MOCHI

U **Uke mochi.** Goddess of food, Ukemochi-no-kami, "Goddess who protects food." If you started your read of this book at the letter A, as most people would, you will remember that Tsukuyami, the brother of Ameratsu, the Sun Goddess, invited to a dinner at the palace of Uke mochi was disgusted when she pulled fish from her mouth when facing the ocean, game when facing the forest, and rice when facing the fields, and food from other parts of her body that we won't mention here. When she finally coughed up a bowl of rice for him to eat, he killed her. Even after she was dead her body kept turning out food and her eyebrows became silkworms. Finding that the food issuing from her could not be destroyed, Tsukuyami took the grains and animals and gave them to Inari, the *Kami* of agriculture, general prosperity and worldly success who, wait for it, was married to Uke mochi or, was Uke mochi, who could be both male and female, and a fox at times. Otogosa-hime, the daughter of Uke mochi, riding on a red goose would descend to put seeds of the crops in the ground, she too was able to get food from any part of her body, horses, oxen, millet, wheat, and beans. This story is also told with another brother of Ameratsu, Susanoo the storm god, taking the place of Tsukuyami. We are dealing with mythology here so don't go looking for logic, there isn't any.

When the string of islands (created in a number of bizarre ways by the gods) off the coast of Korea consolidated into the nation of Japan the various belief systems native to each of the islands intermingled over the centuries. Shinto became the national religion, c.300 BCE-300 CE and gathered up the myths and legends, gods and goddesses that were common to the people. These stories were transmitted orally, there being no written form of Japanese until the Chinese writing system was introduced in the 4th century CE, so it's understandable that characters and stories got mixed up. Ameratsu became the goddess to whom all Shinto Emperors traced their ancestry and Uke mochi got to be a Shinto goddess too.

While she was obviously an important food providing goddess, whether as the wife of Inari or as Inari, she would be a *Kami*. The *Kami* are elements in nature, spirits of the deceased, creationary forces of the universe found in all things. No one word in English expresses the full meaning of *Kami*.

Cool Fact: Izanagi and Izanami, brother and sister twins, were the parents of Uke mochi and Ameratsu. Even though there are Shinto shrines to Uke mochi, she doesn't get the same kind of coverage as some of the other gods and goddesses enshrined in the Shinto religion, perhaps because Tsukuyami killed her.

What other Goddess names start with U?

V is for Venus

Venus. Roman Goddess of luck, love, beauty, desire, sex, fertility, prosperity, and victory, she was associated with cultivated fields and gardens. She represented motherhood and domesticity and was the Mother of Rome. Here's how that came about- Venus seduced Anchis and gave birth to Aeneas who was a Trojan prince, he fled at the fall of Troy, made his way to Italy, and was led to Latium, where Rome was founded, by Venus as the morning star. Well, that's one version. In another, Aeneas is the son of Aphrodite and after arriving in Italy becomes the ancestor of Romulus and Remus, the founders of Rome. The Romans appropriated the Greek pantheon of gods and Venus is their version of Aphrodite. As the Mother of Rome she held a special place in the hearts of Romans, various cults built up around her each with their own temple dedicated to her various roles, having their own rituals and culture. As *Venus Erycina* the Love Goddess, *Venus Cluacina* 'she who purifies as Myrtle', as *Venus Cloacina* she was 'Patroness of the Sewerage System'. Julius Caesar claimed that *Venus Genetrix* was his ancestor and as such, expected to be worshiped as a god, well, we know what happened there. After he was assassinated, his successor, Augustus, claimed both *Venus Genetrix* and *Venus Felix* as his ancestresses, something other leading Romans were in the habit of doing. The month of April, *Veneralia,* was sacred to her, when she shared a wine festival with Jupiter, King of the gods; there were other festivals to her in August and September. Although her temples had statues of her, the most famous of all, the 6'8" tall Venus de Milo, on display in the Louvre Museum in Paris, discovered on the island of Minos in 1820, is more than likely that of Aphrodite. It was in pieces when found and her arms remain missing. The Venus de Medici, a marble copy from the 1st century BC of a bronze original, slightly smaller than the de Milo, completely nude, is considered to be one of the finest sculptures in existence, that too is Aphrodite.

"Venus de Milo was noted for her charms, But, strictly between us, You are cuter than Venus, And what's more you have arms!

"Love is just around the corner" Music by Lewis E. Gensler, Lyrics by Leo Robin, 1934

In the propitiatory gesture, the middle finger, the forefinger, and the thumb are held up together, it was given by Greek and Roman orators before a speech or recital. Jupiter's forefinger for fortunate guidance, Saturn's middle finger for rain, and Venus's thumb for increase. It became the Latin Blessing.

With the advent of Christianity, Venus became, St. Venere.

Cool Fact: The German Goddess Frijjo, Frija, and Frig in Anglo Saxon, became identified with Venus in the early centuries AD, so, *Dies Veneris* "day of Venus" became Frigedag, Friday. Fish, being sacred to both Venus and Frig, had to be eaten on Friday instead of meat, a practice picked up by the Catholic church although, that's no longer required of Roman Catholics in the USA.

What other Goddess names start with V?

W is for Wakka-us-Kamuy

Wakka-us-Kamuy. Ainu Goddess of fresh water, also known as **Petorush Mat** (Watering place Woman). As a benevolent goddess, sympathetic to humans, who oversees the river valleys where the Ainu communities live, she is often petitioned to intercede on their behalf whenever things go bad. In one myth, the cultural hero and sorcerer, Okikurmi, who is also a *Kamuy* (god), asks her on behalf of the Ainu people, to help end a famine that had broken out. She then arranges a feast and invites the *Kamuy* of the rapids, the *Kamuy* of the fish, the *Kamuy* of game, and the goddess of the hunt, Hasinaw-uk Kamuy, (a *kamuy* of great importance to the Ainu who historically subsisted on hunting, fishing and gathering) who wielded a bow and arrows and was accompanied by, or sometimes appeared as, a small bird that showed hunters where to find game. She also invited the overseer of the land, Kotan-kor Kamuy, (not to be confused with **Kotan-kar Kamuy,** the creator deity of plenty and success). Being a skilled singer and dancer, Wakka-us-Kamuy entertained the visitors and once they were relaxed and at ease, she brought up the plight of the humans. The fish *kamuy* says he has locked up all the salmon in his storehouse because the humans were not carrying out the proper rituals when fishing; the game *kamuy* says it was the same for the deer. Kotan-kor Kamuy was also angry they hadn't made offerings to him either. Unbeknownst to the Kamuy feasting, while continuing to dance, the goddess, together with Hasinaw-uk-Kamuy, out of sympathy for the people, sent their souls to the storehouses to release the fish and deer. Afterwards, Wakka-us-Kamuy sent a dream to Okikurmi that explained what happened and why, at the same time warning him that the rituals had to be followed out properly in the future. It's the same message we hear time and again: Don't mess with Mother Nature! When are we going to learn?

The Ainu, much as indigenous peoples elsewhere, were discriminated against by settlers from the mainland, China, Korea, and Russia, who became the Japanese. The Japanese government forbade the use of the Ainu language and customs. The Ainu claim to have been in Japan "a hundred thousand years before the Children of the Sun came". Although of Mongol descent, the Ainu men, beginning at an early age, wear full beards and both sexes are distinctly not Japanese. They have no written language and due to the suppression of the spoken language, Ainu speakers have all but disappeared. Storytelling, such as the one above, has kept the language alive. Government funding and cultural freedom now has allowed the Ainu people to start regaining and preserving their traditions and way of life.

Cool Fact: The first Ainu to enter the Japanese Diet (the governing body consisting of two chambers; the house of Councillors, and the house of Representatives) was Shigeru Kayano, in 1994. He dedicated his life to promoting the well-being and awareness of the Ainu; some Japanese are still unaware of the existence of the Ainu. It was thanks to him, and other supporters, that the policy of extinction by assimilation and the law forbidding their culture, was finally lifted in 1997.

What other Goddess names start with W?

X IS FOR XI WANG MU

Xi Wang mu. Great Goddess of China. Queen Mother of the West. The difficulties in translating one language into another makes determining the true name of Xi Wang mu (Hsi Wang Mu) a matter of "take your pick". *Wangmu* means "grandmother" but it can be applied to female ancestors while *wang* can denote spirits of any kind. We do know she is one of the oldest deities of China, she resembles a human but has tiger's teeth and a leopard's tail. As a tigress, she is connected to Shamanism, the stool she sits on, her headdress, and staff, which are still part of a shaman's paraphernalia in Taiwan, confirm the connection. Her head ornament, shown in some illustrations, a horizontal band with flares at the end, is usually interpreted as a symbol of the loom, marking her as the cosmic weaver of the universe. She ordains death, disease, and healing. She is attended by a host of spirits and transcendentals. Presiding over the dead and the afterlife, she confers divine realization and immortality on spiritual seekers. In her garden, hidden by high clouds, on the Kunlun Mountains, peaches of immortality grow on a colossal tree, ripening only once every 3000yrs. The tree connects heaven and earth and serves as a ladder for spirits and shamans to reach her. In one legend the Zho dynasty king Mu (circa 1000 BCE) was granted an audience at which time she presented him with five peaches. He wanted to save the seeds for planting but she told him that they would not bear fruit for 3000yrs. New religions and beliefs came along through the ages and she was worked into each of them as the common people revered her too much to let her go. During an uprising in the Han dynasty, she was seen by the peasantry as the one who would create "a world where all would be equal." The revolt was put down but change was in the air. The later Han dynasty set up altars to Xi Wang mu as a gesture to the people. The courtly writers turned her from a wild-haired shamanic goddess into a lady with aristocratic robes and jeweled headdresses. Confucianism and Taoism couldn't change her although she was shown flying through the heavens to worship Buddha and the Han elite even invented a husband for her but, that did not find favor among the populace. Two thousand years later she was being partnered with the goddess of the Eastern Sea as well as with another, The Sovereign of the Dawn Cloud. Through it all, she remained the Queen Mother for, though she met with Emperors, she was the traditional guardian of women and girls, particularly those outside the family system; singers, dancers, prostitutes, nuns, hermits, and sages who attained the Tao, were her special proteges. The idea of "all being equal" didn't gain traction until Chairman Mao came along but I don't think he gives her any credit in his Little Red Book (the brainchild of Lin Biao, a decorated general in the Liberation Army and Mao's heir apparent).

Cool Fact: Xi Wang mu, with all her goddess capabilities and features, tiger's teeth and all, her immense powers and fighting skills, is one of the boss characters in the Japanese PlayStation game, **Strider** (2014).

What other Goddess names start with X?

Y IS FOR YHI

Y **Yhi, Yarai, Yaay. Yhi** is the creation goddess of the Gamilarray people of New South Wales and southwest Queensland, Australia. The goddess of light and a solar deity. She created everything; here's how the people tell the story (they also have a creator ancestor god but, we are not dealing with that here.) Yhi lived in the Dreamtime, a word that has been given various meanings but in simple terms, is a time and place outside of this world. Yhi was sleeping when a whistle woke her up, when she opened her eyes light fell upon the earth which, at the time, was no more than a bleak, barren orb. She decided, as most women would, that it needed to be 'fixed up.' As she walked across the earth plants grew up in her wake and in no time the whole world was covered in foliage. She then wanted to make something that could dance. Looking around, she found evil spirits living underground who tried to sing her to death but her warmth and light dispelled their darkness and all kinds of insects followed her out into the light in a dancing mass and went to commune with the plants and flowers. She then found some ice caves in a mountain and when she shone her light inside, fishes and lizards emerged and went to the lakes and rivers made by the ice her warmth had melted. From the other caves she visited, all kinds of birds, animals, and amphibians rushed into the sunlight. Blessing her creations with the change of seasons, she returned to the Dreamtime promising them that when they died they would join her there. As she disappeared, darkness fell and all the creatures were sad thinking she would never return, then the first sunrise came and Yhi had returned, as she would do every morning. After many millennia, Yhi sensed that the animals were not happy, she asked them what was wrong and the Kangaroo said that it really wanted to jump, the Wombat said it wanted to wiggle on the ground, the Seal wanted to swim, Lizard wanted legs and Bat wanted wings, and the Platypus wanted a bit of everything. Yhi granted their wishes and returned to the sky, there she realized that the Man, who was unlike any of her other creations, didn't have a woman. Yhi turned all her power onto a flower while the man was sleeping, when he awoke, he watched, along with the rest of the other creatures, as the flower turned into a woman. This is just one of the many stories that are told, sung, acted out, and danced to remind the people of their shared heritage.

The Australian Aboriginals arrived on the continent about 70,000 years ago. There are 250 distinct language groups although in some cases there are only a handful of people who speak their tribal language. It is estimated that between 750,000 and 1.25 million were living there when the British colonists arrived. As elsewhere, imported epidemics ravaged the natives, settlers seized their land, and those that resisted died in violent conflicts, massacres, and impoverishment killed many more. Yhi still returns every morning and the people still celebrate her coming.

Cool Fact: Found only on Orpheus Island, Queensland which is a National Park, near the Great Barrier Reef, the amphipod crustacean, **Yhi yindi** was named by J. Laurens Barnard and J. O. Thomas in 1991. It is the only species in the genus **Yhi**.

What other Goddess names start with Y?

Z is for Zemyna

Z **Zemyna, Zemynele, Zemele.** Lithuanian earth goddess. Zeme- earth in Lithuanian. Another Mother Goddess, there's just a lot of them out there. In the Baltic region there are at least seventy goddesses with 'Mother' attached to their name, each with something distinct to mother; flowers, livestock, the sea, earth, wind, and fire, and lest we forget, Mother of Mushrooms. Zemyna is the personification of the fertile earth, she nurtures all life, human, plant, and animal. Since all that is born will die, she is also the goddess of the dead. Lithuania was the last pagan country in Europe to convert to Christianity. Conversion started in the 13th century but whether to go Greek Orthodox or Roman Catholic led to a very violent, drawn-out process during which pagan practices persisted. Even after Lithuania became officially Christian in the 15th century, paganism held sway with the peasantry and it wasn't until the 17th century when the majority of people were Christian that pagan temples were destroyed and Zemyna became identified with the Virgin Mary. Despite being described as a virgin in both the Bible and the Quran, (she is mentioned more often in the Quran than in the Bible) Mary was also called the Mother of God so, although not being associated with the earth, her role as a mother was enough to tie her to Zemyna and vice versa. Rituals performed at weddings, at harvest time or other major celebrations were dedicated to her with prayers and libations being spilled on the ground by the head of the household, the sacrifice of a chicken that would then be eaten by the family after which, the bones and scrapes would be burned or buried as offerings to Zemyna. Before the sowing of new crops in the Spring, bread made from flour of the previous year's crop would be buried in the field to be seeded. At the yearly harvest feast, a black suckling piglet was offered by a Priestess. Grave consequences could be expected if offerings were not made at regular intervals. As usual with fertility earth goddesses, Zemyna was also associated with death. People kissed the earth in recognition that one day they would return to her, their ruler and guardian. The earth, her domain, in Lithuanian folklore, being the final abode of humankind. Nijole Laurinkiene wrote in her book, *Zemyna and her mythical world* that when a child was born; "the newborn would immediately be laid down on Mother Earth as if she were its biological mother so that she could 'accept' and 'embrace' the infant as her own earthly creation and give it vegetative power and vitality on a cosmic plane." Two mothers are better than one.

Cool Fact: Romuva is an organization that has revived Paganism in Lithuania and its founder is seeking to have it recognized as an official religion. Romuva is named for a temple of tranquility that, according to legend, existed in the pre-medieval period of Lithuanian history.

What other Goddess names start with Z?

Nanu Buluko

Bonus

Some sources will state that Lahamu, the firstborn daughter of Tiamat and Apsu, and her brother, Lahmu were the parents of Anshar and Kisha who were the parents of the first gods. Well, how could that be, since their parents and grandparents were gods and goddesses? My research has shown me that many such statements continue to be printed without question, and just as likely contradicted in the next paragraph. Don't get upset or try to figure it all out, just go along for the ride, you will definitely be entertained. Tiamat, also known as Nammu, was the Akkadian goddess of Creative Chaos, everything originated from her primeval waters from which she arose to give birth to the earth, heaven, and the first gods. Apsu was the god of sweet water and the Heavenly Oceans of Wisdom. Tiamat's salty sea waters were very bitter so, when she and Apsu joined up their waters made a pleasant blend. The Akkadian Empire is considered to be the first in the world, it became an empire by conquering Sumer, a far older civilization of non-Semitic people who had settled along the Tigris and Euphrates Rivers around 6000BCE. Later, Sargon the Great united all the Semitic-speaking people from the Persian Gulf to the Mediterranean and in so doing, helped the spread of the stories of Akkadian and Sumerian gods and goddesses throughout the Middle East. The acts of those gods and goddesses became attributed to each people's own gods, the great flood of the Sumerians, created by An and Enlil, who had gotten fed up with mankind, though it may have been caused by a tsunami in the Persian Gulf, was picked up by others, most famously the Hebrews who attributed it to their god. How far back these stories go, we will never know. Did the gods create humans or did humans create the gods? Just like the eternal question, the chicken or the egg, these questions might as well be dropped; just enjoy them for what they are; attempts to explain, in sometimes extremely imaginative ways, how this world came about. We will likely never know when the idea developed, that a goddess, perhaps with the aid of a god, created this earth and all that lives here, it's been around for thousands, perhaps hundreds of thousands of years. Our task is to try to ensure that those who inherit this amazing world continue to enjoy what is left of her gifts.

Cool Fact: Africa is called the cradle of Mankind so, we may have found the original goddess! Nanu Buluko, Nana Buruku, etc. Supreme Goddess, Mother of all Mothers. She appears as an old woman who is the creator of the world, her twin children, Lisa and Mawu, are the sun and the moon. She is the most revered deity in West Africa, shared, under different names, by many ethnic groups, some of which worship her while others worship the gods that originate from her. She traveled to the Americas along with enslaved West Africans and is now found in Brazil, French, Dutch, and British West Indies and throughout the Caribbean.

More A to Z Goddesses.

A. Aditi, Aine, Akycha, Athena, Artemis, Amphitrite, An, Ashtoreth, Asibikaashi.
B. Bastet, Beset, Badb, Bast, Baubo, Blodewedd, Branwen.
C. Coyolxuahqui, Cybele, Cuaxolotl, Ceres, Clemencia, Cerridwen, Coventina.
D. Diana, Dewi, Ratih, Danu, Dike, Discordia, Djanggawui.
E. Eris, Edda, Eos, Eleh, Epona, Erishkigal, Eirene.
F. Flora, Frigg, Faustitus, Fand, Fachea, Febris, Fand, Flidais.
G. Gaia, Geshtin, Ga-Tum-Dug, Gula, Gefion, Gerdr.
H. Hathor, Hel, Hera, Hauhet, Hina, Hekaolas, Henwen, Hebe, Hekate.
I. Inanna, Isis, Ixtab, Idun, Ishtar, Iris, Isanamij.
J. Jiang Yuan, Jingwei, Juno, Juventas, Jiu tian Xuannu.
K. Kali, Ki, Kauket, Kuan Yin, Kayra, Khione, Kamira.
L. La'aka, Lakshmi, Luna, Leto, Levana, Lissa.
M. Morrigan, Minerva, Maia, Maeve, Maat, Mamimitu, Maliya.
N. Nephthys, Nemesis, Nyx, Nut, Naunet, Nasr, Nike, Nu Gua, Nisaba.
O. Oizys, Olwen, Ostara, Onatah.
P. Pomona, Persephone, Parvati, Phoebe, Pax.
Q. Qa, Qamai'ts, Q'orianka.
R. Rumina, Renpet, Rhiannon, Remi, Remnit, Rujula, Rhapso.
S. Satet, Sekhmet, Sajna, Sengu-Sama, Saraswati, Seshat, Selene.
T. Tiamat, Theia, Themis, Tethys, Thalia, Tyche, Trishika.
U. Uni, Ulfran, Uma, Urania, Uelanuhi.
V. Vesta, Vellana, Veritas, Vaishu, Vei.
W. Wuriupranili, Wala, Wurusema.
X. Xilonen, Xochiquetzal, Xihe, Xanthe, Xatel-Ekwa.
Y. Yaghuth, Ya'uq, Yushkep Kamuy, Yemaya.
Z. Zabi, Ziva, Zelena, Zara-Mama, Zaria, Zemele.

Bibliography

Graves, Robert. *The White Goddess.* Farrar, Straus and Giroux 1948
Mascetti, Manuela Dunn. *The Song of Eve.* Simon & Schuster NY 1990
Philip, Neil. DK Annotated Guides *Myths and Legends.* DK Publishing NY 1999
Philips, Tony and Charles. *The Great Thymes.* Duncan Baird Publishers London 2000
Michailidou, Anna. *Knossos* Ekdotike Athenon SA Athens 1986
Goodison, Lucy, & Morris, Christine, Editors. *Ancient Goddesses* U. Of Wisconsin Press, Wis. 1998
Leeming, David Adams. *The World of Myth.* Oxford University Press 1990
Sitchin, Zecharia. *The Lost Realms* and, *When Time Began.* Avon Press NY 1990 & 1993
Larouse Encyclopedia of Mythology Prometheus Press NY 1959
Kelly, Lynne. *The Memory Code* Atlantic Press 2017
Wikipedia.com
Mythopedia.com
Mythologysource.com
Mexicounexplained.com
Worldhistory.org.
The Japanese Gallery for Amateratsu. Duncan Baird Publishers
Acknowledgements:
Heimdall returns the necklace. Nils Blommer (1846)
Ix Chel https://www.gods-and-goddesses.com
Hopi Woman by unknown author-https://www.crystalinks.com
Mnemosyne:https://greekgodsandgoddesses.net & /venus
www.originalbotanica.com
babalawoweb.com
yagbeoniln.com
Painting by David Howard Hitchcock c. 1929
Stele of Quetesh/Kadesh Dynasty XIX91292-1186BCE) Museo Egizio photo by Jalsanna Lee- https://plus.google.com/photo
thaliatook.com
Rhea- Pergamonmuseum
tofugu.com/japan/ainu-japan
kasijbaik.blogspot.com
Max dashu suppressedhistory.net/goddess/xiwangmu.html
catalystmagazine.net/profile-of-a-goddess/yhi/

Collect All of the A to Z Books!

The A to Z Book of Birds
The A to Z Book of Cats
The A to Z Book of Did You Know
The A to Z Book of Gods
The A to Z Book of Goddesses
The A to Z Book of Mushrooms
The A to Z Book of Turtle Island
The A to Z Book of Weeds
The A to Z Book of Wildflowers

Also Check out his Other Books

Alga and Kevin
Be Not Deceived
Corpus

Magic Faces – Caras Magicas

Reviews: If you enjoyed this book, Michael P. Earney would appreciate it if you would leave a review on Amazon, Goodreads, or any other Review site you like.

Also, don't forget to tell your friends! Word of mouth advertising is the most precious *"Thank You"* a reader can ever give an author.

About the Author: Michael P. Earney is a fine arts painter who grew up in England. His writer's voice reflects curiosity and passion for the world of nature. His text is instructive yet playful. The illustrations are executed with grace and fine detail. Earney is in his element as artist, writer, educator, and naturalist. To learn more about this author's books and various achievements please visit his websites.

Contact Mr. Earney: themichaelearney@yahoo.com
Websites: www.MichaelEarney.com and www.EarneyWorks.com
Publisher: www.ErinGoBraghPublishing.com/authors/mearney

www.ingramcontent.com/pod-product-compliance
Lightning Source LLC
Chambersburg PA
CBHW040338120426
42742CB00046BA/56